JOHN THOMPSON'S
EASIEST PIANO COURSE

FIRST BEETHOVEN

Arranged by Christopher Hussey

ISBN 978-1-4950-6612-2

WILLIS MUSIC

EXCLUSIVELY DISTRIBUTED BY

HAL•LEONARD®
CORPORATION

Visit Hal Leonard Online at
www.halleonard.com

Ode to Joy

Ludwig van Beethoven

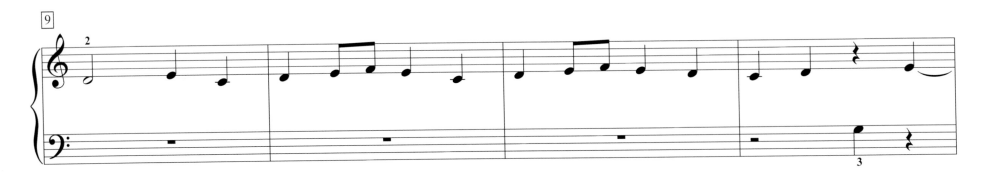

Rondo in C

Ludwig van Beethoven

Moderato e grazioso

Turkish March

Ludwig van Beethoven

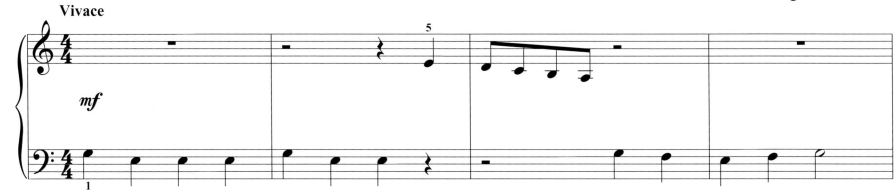

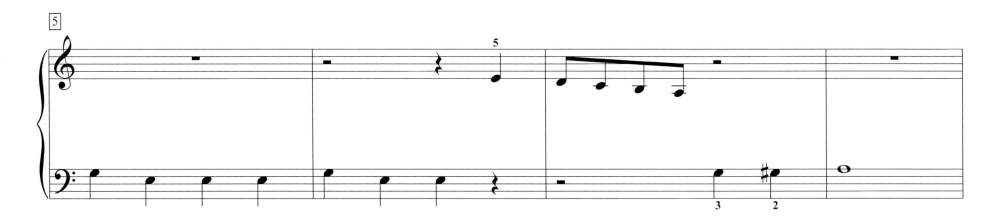

Sonatina in G Major

Ludwig van Beethoven

Chorus of Prisoners

Allegro ma non troppo

Ludwig van Beethoven

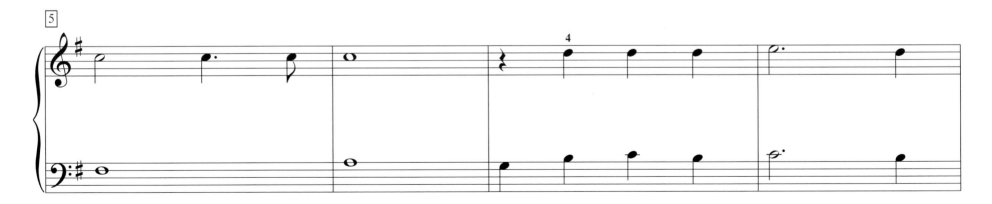

Piano Sonata No. 25

Ludwig van Beethoven

Symphony No. 5

Ludwig van Beethoven

Allegro con brio

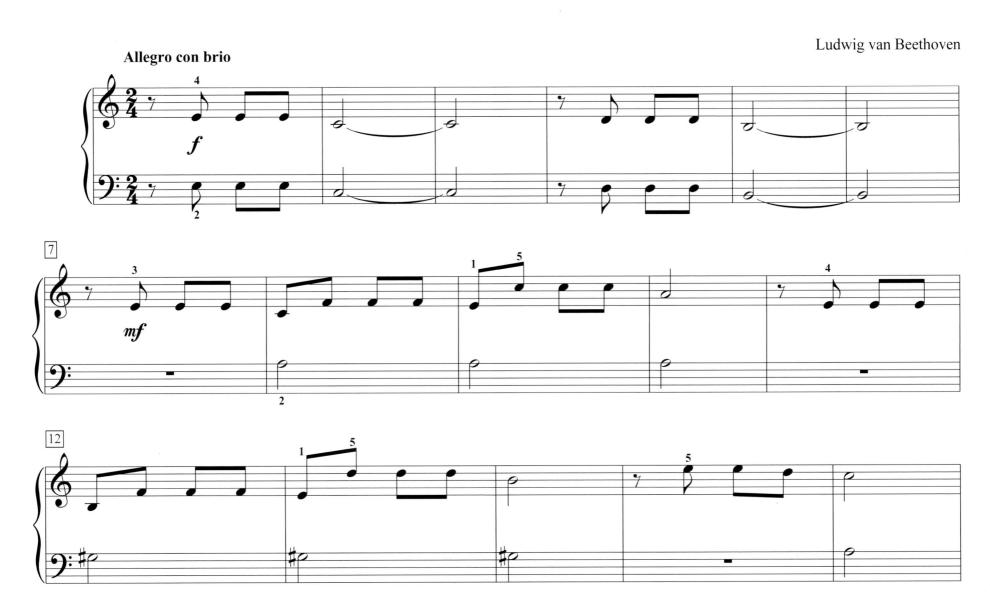

Symphony No. 6
("Pastoral")

Ludwig van Beethoven

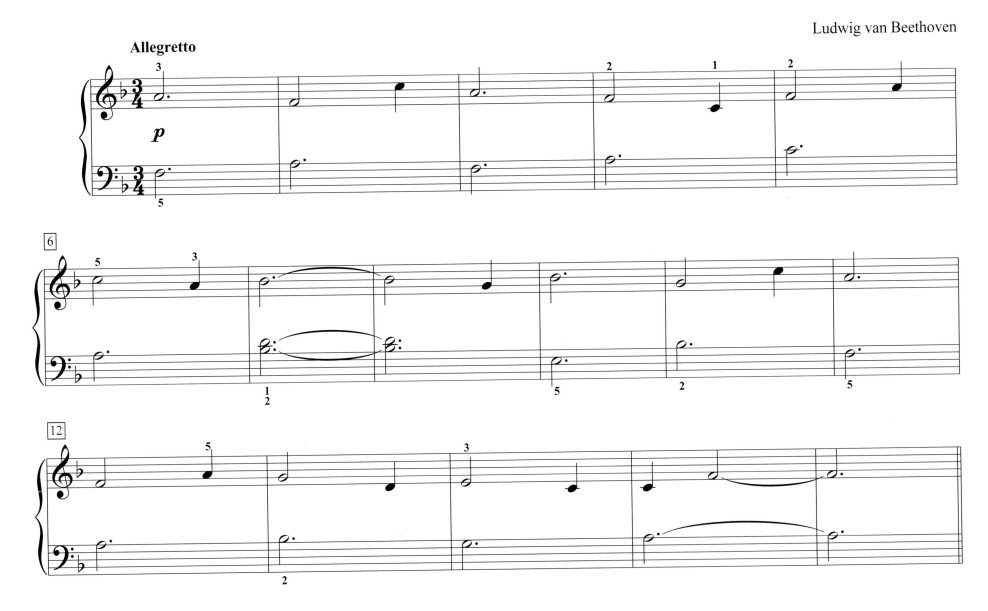

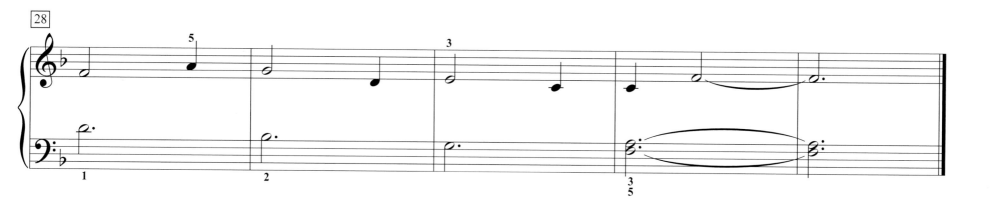

Moonlight Sonata

Ludwig van Beethoven

Adagio sostenuto

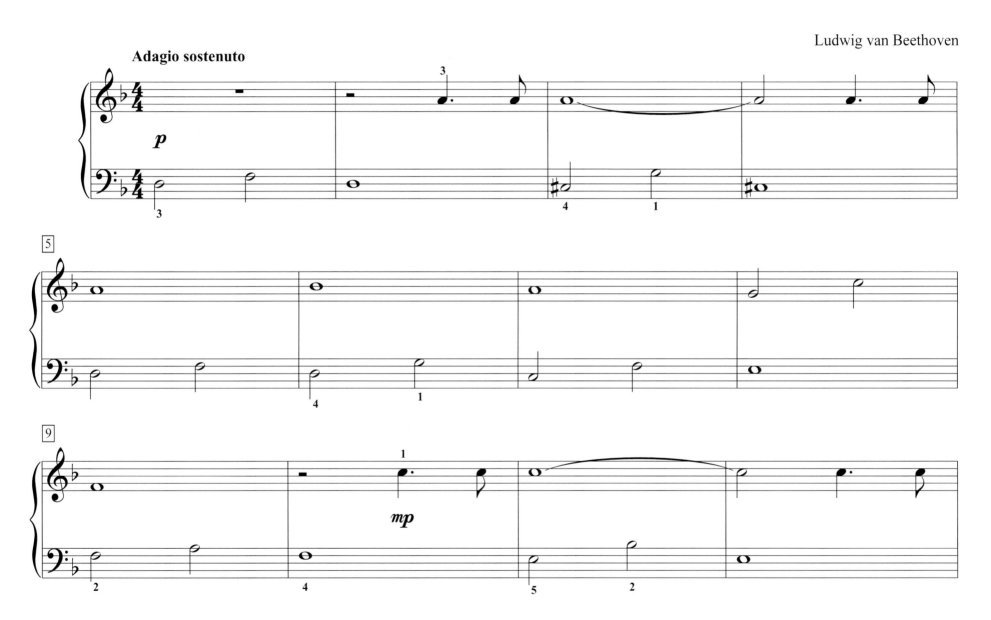

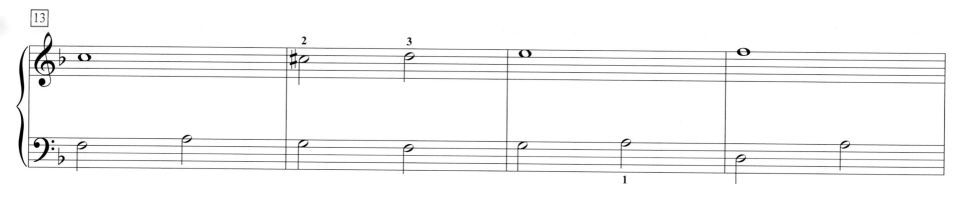

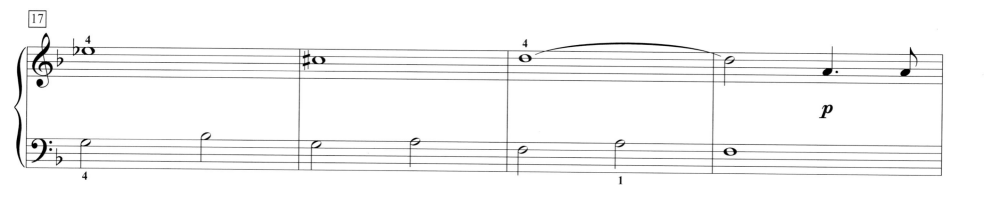

Symphony No. 3
("Eroica")

Ludwig van Beethoven

Allegro con brio

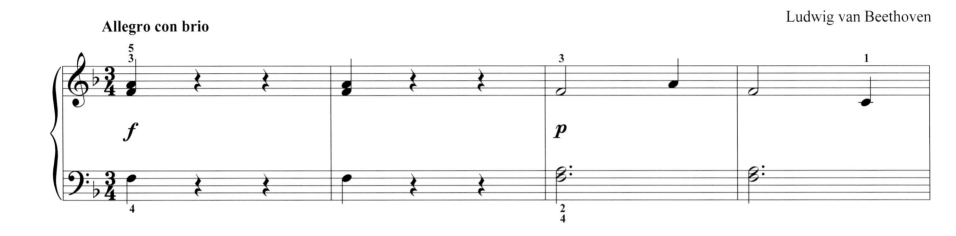

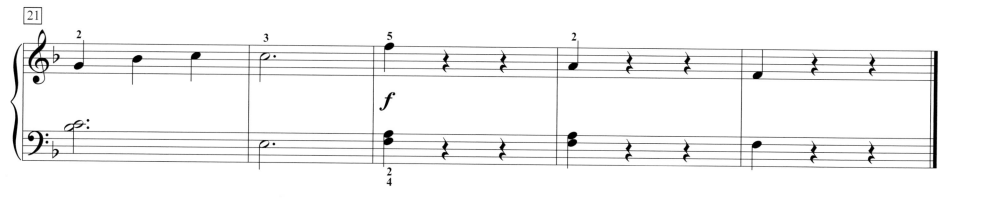

Rage Over a Lost Penny

Ludwig van Beethoven

Symphony No. 7

Ludwig van Beethoven

Für Elise

Ludwig van Beethoven

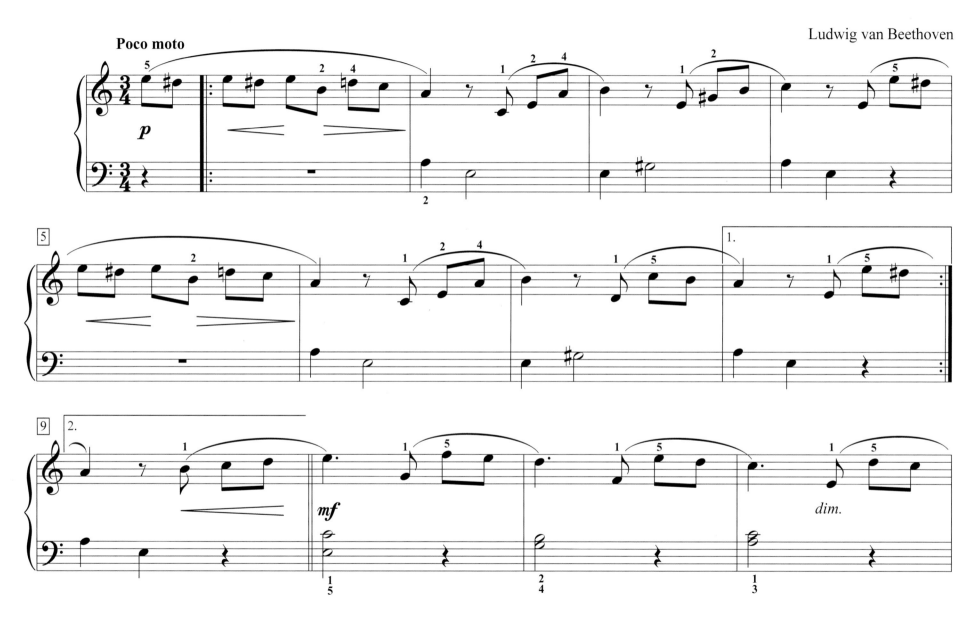

Sonata Pathétique

Ludwig van Beethoven

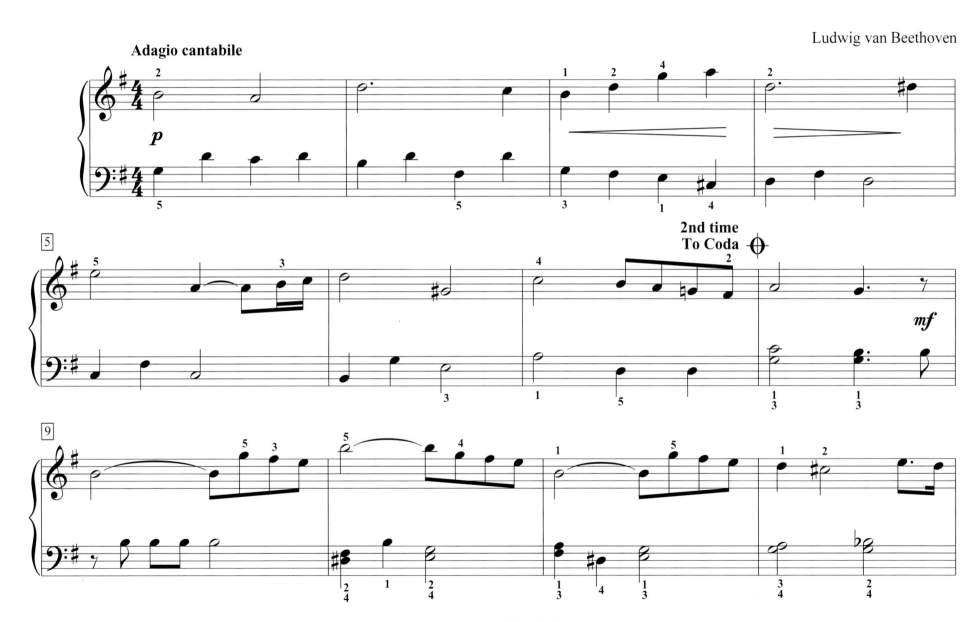

Minuet in G Major

Ludwig van Beethoven

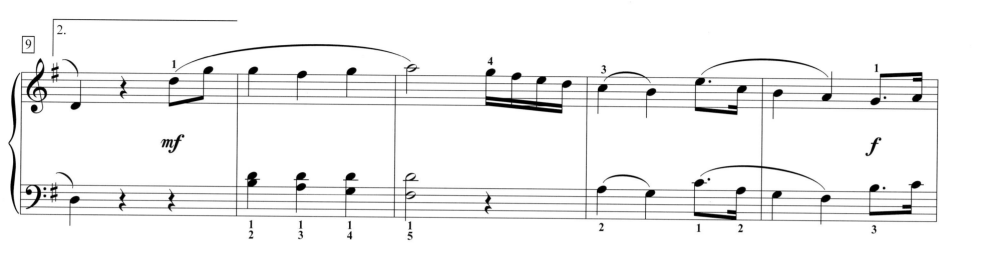

JOHN THOMPSON'S
EASIEST PIANO COURSE

Fun repertoire books are available as an integral part of **John Thompson's Easiest Piano Course.** Graded to work alongside the course, these pieces are ideal for pupils reaching the end of Part 2. They are invaluable for securing basic technique as well as developing musicality and enjoyment.

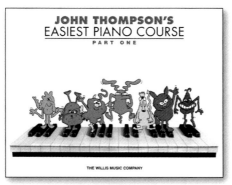

John Thompson's Easiest Piano Course

00414014 Part 1 – Book only $6.99
00414018 Part 2 – Book only $6.99
00414019 Part 3 – Book only $6.99
00414112 Part 4 – Book only $6.99

First Pop Songs *arr. Miller*
00416954................................... $8.99

First Classics
00406347................................... $6.99

First Disney Songs *arr. Miller*
00416880................................... $9.99

First Jazz Tunes *arr. Baumgartner*
00120872................................... $7.99

First Beethoven *arr. Hussey*
00171709................................... $7.99

First Chart Hits
00141171................................... $7.99

Also available:

First Mozart *arr. Hussey*
00171851...................................$7.99

First Nursery Rhymes
00406229...................................$6.99

First Worship Songs *arr. Austin*
00416892...................................$8.99

Prices, contents and availability subject to change without notice.   Disney characters and artwork © Disney Enterprises Inc.   View complete songlists on **www.halleonard.com**

0218